# MY
# TOMORROW
# BECAME
# TODAY

*(A Collection of Inspirational Writings)*

BY

MICHELLE R. PALMER

# Table of Contents

# DEDICATION

★ ★ ★

This book is dedicated to you with immeasurable love:

Ricky Palmer (Husband)

L. Yvonne Reid Garvin (Mother) and Family

Ashley Palmer (Daughter)

Justin and Kaley Palmer (Son and Daughter-in-Law)

Jordan, Alana and Chanel (Grandkids)

Traci Durham (Sister) and Family

The Reid Family

The Palmer Family

The Brinson Family

The White Family

To my eternal supporters, love never dies:

Joe Brinson (Father)

Willie Mae Reid (Grandmother)

Oscar Reid Sr. (Grandfather)

Ruth "Fruit" Brinson (Grandmother)

Dr. Lolita Palmer (Mother-in-Law)

Roland Palmer Sr. (Father-in-Law)

*Thank You God for the Gift of Words!*

*"I will walk my path with more wisdom and frequently stop to pick up flowers along the way. Sometimes these flowers will have thorns while other times they will have blooms. Either way, I'll pick them up with hope and grace." Michelle R. Palmer*

# PREFACE

— ★ ★ ★ —

There are so many things that I want to say but I have a hard time writing it all down. My mind is full of words, poems and essays! However, I have a fear that my gift of writing is still asleep. We've all heard the familiar quote that if you don't use your talent, you might lose your gift. I have not written anything in years.

So now I seek to find the hidden voice within me that hesitates to be noticed. It's hard to explain every single joy, pain and success that happened in my life. But I know that someday when I'm not paying attention, I will hear the words to jumpstart my creativeness.

When this happens, I will be there to scribe every smile, fear and crazy thing that the voice will be revealing to me to write. I believe that the words will just come cascading down to me syllable by syllable. A writer is only a vehicle that the voice uses to travel down the road of experiences. The voice is yearning to wake up and reveal what needs to be said in my story.

Everyone has a story to tell. Our stories are our experiences. We could frantically wake up from a dream that we were terminally ill (and that dream is true). We could wake up from a night of grieving about losing a loved one. We could wake up from crying all night because our spouse asked for a divorce.

However, we woke up today with the fulfillment of being blessed and content. We also have stories to share because we live one day at a time. We've learned to take baby steps because we see something different every time we wipe fog from a window. The clear circle that we peep through leads us to whatever is on the other side.

## MOTIVATE YOURSELF (FALL DOWN/GET BACK UP)

We fall down just to get up again. Life deals us cards that are symbolic to our fate. We gamble everyday with our challenges. We stumble and sometimes we fall. But, over time, we manage to stand up straight and start walking to that next opportunity. Then obstacles appear and they slow us down to the point of feeling helpless. When this happens, vulnerability creeps into our confidence and we lose sight of our goals. Sooner or later, we manage to get back on track. Faith, grace and perseverance give us the strength of empowerment to overcome every setback. We fall down, but we manage to get back up again.

*hope*

# LET THE BLESSINGS FLOW

I've always felt that we'd be blessed with a richness that no man could take away from us. It's a richness that only God can provide to us in the form of financial freedom and a peaceful mind. I've prayed for these things for quite some time. Am I selfish? No, I can ask our creator for these things because he is the provider.

Financial freedom does not necessarily mean that God will give me millions of dollars. I've learned that God can provide us financial freedom so that we don't have to be concerned about when or how the bills will be paid. I believe that this prayer was answered a long time ago. I'm already seeing things changing in our financial sphere. The blessings have started to surface.

As for a peaceful mindset, I've asked for this blessing but I've been my worst enemy. I have some issues that will take time to resolve the layers of problems that have surmounted over the years. I need to laugh more and worry less. I am not afraid of change but I am afraid to fail.

However, I am thankful for the journey that I am experiencing because I've become humble and have learned that mistakes are a part of life. We are not perfect but we must always strive to be better. So today, I've decided to continue this journey with a different attitude because I will get to the next level. Perhaps not when I want to get there but according to God's plan and time. Today I thank God for the blessings that are to come!

## RENEW YOUR MIND

Here I sit underneath my umbrella at New Smyrna Beach and the sky is ever so blue. The clouds are clear and I hear the soothing sound of the waves moving with confidence as they pound upon the shore. The hue of the water is defined by what's underneath the surface. The depth dictates the colorful patterns that I can see from the shoreline.

The ocean is one of the free gifts that we still have access to. It's a place of refuge and a place to de-stress. We've been here for over an hour and my heart rate is calm. I feel like I just completed a good sleep and can't believe how the beach can help one to relax. I feel like there are no worries and fears in my life.

As I sit here in eighty-seven degrees, sun-scorching weather, I squint my eyes to search for my purpose. I desire to hear the ocean and smell the sea. Life is peculiar. One day we are on top of the world and the next day, we realize that we don't have a game. I sit here listening to the tides hit the shore and I think of how the old things must become new again.

I yearn for a good laugh, one that makes your stomach muscles ache and you're out of breath! I haven't laughed in a long time. In fact, I might have forgotten how to laugh. I think it's due to the hurt, fear and pain that has settled within me. I've come to the conclusion that I had it all wrong about my career and assets. They do not define who I am. It sometimes takes a major setback to make you humble.

I look around and observe people playing volleyball on the beach. I sense a freedom attitude amongst them. They volley the ball back and forth with confidence that the person on the other side of the net will miss the ball. There's nothing in between about this game. It's all about hitting and missing the ball.

*hope*

When we take time to relax, we find our minds clearing up the stress that had settled in the space of our conscience. We need to inhale the positives and exhale the negatives. When we take time out to regroup, it's all about having a fresh start. Each time the waves end their cycle, another group of waves form and the cycle starts all over again.

There's nothing like hearing the waves splash over and over again. It's one directional with a unique flow of water and air that causes the waves to succumb to the shore.

Living the moment is the renewed level that I yearn for. We have yesterday behind us because today is here. As I sit here looking toward the ocean, I am in a peaceful state. I long to stay in this element because it feels so good!

# TOMORROW

When things happen in your life that you have no control over, keep looking up to God.

Sometimes our lives are turned completely upside down and we feel victimized but we keep on looking up to God.

Our jobs were outsourced, we lost loved ones to cancer and material things were no longer important. We kept our eyes on God. We've shed tears, had our self-esteem "messed with," and we lost sleep over fears of not having money. But our eyes were focused on God seeing us through.

It didn't mean that we were being punished or that we lacked faith and security. Life is all about opportunities for us to pass through our season. No matter what, temptation and disappointment will surface during one of our seasons. However, we must always look up to God because he never sleeps. So, don't worry. Tomorrow will always take care of itself.

*hope*

# TEARS OF HOPE (MY SOUL CRIED OUT)

I cried my soul out to God. I am entitled to happiness and peace. No situation has the authority to steal my joy because I am blessed.

My soul cried out for a peaceful state to wrap my entire body and calm my inner-being.

I am like a thought that never really sleeps. I constantly yearn for a better way to sort through issues.

To experience a corporate layoff as a married couple can be brutal to the marriage and finances. We worked for the same company for over twenty years and our jobs were downsized. Through our faith, love and friendship, we partnered together through this storm and made it work. So, my cries today are for others that will go through a similar situation. My friends, you are entitled to happiness and peace. No situation has the authority to steal your joy because You Are Blessed!

## MY EULOGY

If my life ends tonight, I have not lived in vain.

Do not cry for my soul because I know God. He's been there throughout my journey. Every step and every hurdle. Every breath of joy and laughter, as well as each challenge and sad season.

I have lived within a united marriage and created beautiful children that have grown up to become productive citizens in our crazy world.

It took some time, but I finally realized that the beach is a spiritual place to connect to God. It's my creative and reflective place.

I have not lived in vain because I understand that there are no promised tomorrows. I've had my share of worries but my needs have always been met. My loved ones are always in my heart and prayers. I believe that God will keep us together as one.

hope

# SHE'S ALL THAT

She parks the car and tilts the mirror to view her make-up one more time

She smiles as she sees the wrinkles near her eyes

She looks at her dimpled checks and glances at her aged neckline

Then she compliments herself for aging with grace.

As she opens the car door, she feels her aching muscles

That won't deter her from getting out of the car

She's survived a health crisis with strength and resilience

It did not steal her joy!

She adjusts her clothes as her feet touch the pavement

Then she walks with a stride of confidence because she's comfortable in her skin

As she approaches the front of the building, she loudly chuckles to herself, "I am all that!"

# WORDS OF ENCOURAGEMENT

For many decades, I did not listen to my writer's voice because I was busy trying to control my destiny. I encourage others to slow down and embrace life's treasures. Recognize the clear thoughts of things you might want to do. The desires might be dormant for years, but will resurface when you least expect them to appear. Just be still for a moment so that you can find your purpose.

We all have a purpose in life. There are many talents that were given to us. We just get caught up in the day-to-day activities that we ignore the gems. A fallen diamond might be right next to our foot, but we're so focused on issues that don't see the gem on the ground. That gem could have been a missed opportunity.

Sometimes a missed opportunity will resurface years later. When this happens, grab ahold of it and take it to the next level. Don't be dismayed about what didn't happen and don't be afraid to embrace your blessings. Just acknowledge and embrace the gift that was uniquely made for you.

*hope*

# GLASS HALF EMPTY AND HALF FULL

I have walked a long path full of discoveries, joy, solitude and pain. I've learned not to take things for granted. I've seen beautiful sunsets and hurricane destructions in the same day. I've smelled sweet flowers and rotten garbage in the same area. I've hated and loved someone in the same moment. I have laughed and been laughed at in the same instance. I'm definitely as human as the next person that has lived a life as full and half-empty as mine.

## A CHANGE IS COMING

I often get excited when I think about new beginnings. There was a time when I would hesitate or talk myself out of embarking on new ventures. However, I have developed inner confidence that confirms it is O.K. to have big aspirations. Age has no barrier on achievements.

Faith gives us the courage to not give up. We must remember that the ground is beneath us when we leap out on faith. We don't need to hesitate or hope for a distraction. However, we must stay focused, be confident and look straight ahead. We should jump with open arms to embrace our new beginnings before we land.

*hope*

# VICTIMS OF CIRCUMSTANCE

We will experience times in our lives when we feel that we are victims. We might be unhappy and are fiercely searching for a better tomorrow. We pray to God for guidance but we become impatient because he does not answer us right away. Then, we become preoccupied with looking for a Godly sign that he heard our prayers. We even try to take over God's role by solving our own issues.

This is an indication that we're lacking faith. Like many of you, I've been guilty of not trusting in God to answer my prayers. We must be ready when he does answer our prayers. I can attest that God has opened my soul and revealed my weaknesses and fears. It's occurred when I least expected it. The communication might be an incident or someone might offer unsolicited advice. It could be a phone call or an unexpected financial gift.

I encourage you to observe the unexpected things that you refer to as luck. God doesn't deliver luck; however, he does deliver the answers to your prayers. When you embrace the signs and take action, it will help you overcome feeling like you are a victim of the circumstance.

# WE ARE GOD'S CHILDREN

We must not judge any man by his pigmentation because every skin color is perfect. Our uniqueness is greater than our similarities. God purposely made us different. We have our own fingerprints, footprints and dental records as indicators that we all are God's children with differences. There's no reason for hatred or judgement. We are all God's children!

hope

# FREEDOM

I yearn to swing open a large door that overlooks the ocean. When this occurs, I want to take a giant inhalation of enriched sea air! As I exhale, I want to never look back at the could've, should've and would've situations. I want a renewed mind that has been rejuvenated and strengthened to deal with all obstacles that might come my way. This renewed feeling is waiting for the moment that I embrace it!

# PANDEMIC REFLECTIONS

On my recent trip to the beach, I discovered an impeccable feeling of releasing anxiety, fear, sadness, doubt and pain. As I approached the water, the tide was high and both feet became a part of the ocean's edge. Embedded feet in the sand made me feel grounded, in balance and confident again.

The 2020-2021 pandemic affected me in different ways. I survived covid-19. Like others, I've lost loved ones due to covid-19 and other illnesses. Each loss added a layer of sadness to my inner being. Coping with it has been a challenge. However, my faith is still strong.

I've tried not to be judgmental. We're all different and yet very similar when it comes to our beliefs that we learned from our parents, friends and the communities we are a part of. No one is perfect but we seem to get stuck on what we think is right. We need to truthfully ask ourselves who is it right for because we can no longer lie to ourselves and others.

It is not acceptable to have hatred in your heart. It's also not acceptable to look the other way. It's not acceptable to hide behind religion. Most of all, it's not acceptable for us (as a whole) to not be OK. I encourage each person to renew his/her mind and think outside of the box. That's a big step towards healing.

*hope*

# A PRAISE DANCER'S MESSAGE

I don't dance for fame or recognition

I dance for joy

I dance for strength

I dance for healing

I dance for deliverance!

# JOE COOL

My father was a handsome, cool man. He was a sharp dresser that looked good in fedora hats. A man that loved fishing and loved women. I was a little girl when I met him. He didn't raise me but we had a great relationship. I never called him dad. I called him Joe. If Joe had told me to call him dad, I would have. But he never did. Sometimes it felt more like he was my uncle because he never disciplined me. But I respected him as my father.

When I visited him in New York, I shared him with everyone. His family was large and he commanded everyone's attention. He was the life of the party.

By living a carefree life, one experiences happiness, sadness, togetherness and separations.

Seasons come and go. For Joe, the months changed to years and time fast forwarded quickly. Before we knew it, Joe was an old man. The decades passed and Joe's health declined and he had to reside in a skilled nursing home that was six hours drive from my house. Many family members and friends visited him, so he was never alone. I was determined to see him but quite uncomfortable that the visit might not go well.

Our phone conversations had become one directional. I asked questions and he briefly answered them. So, this is why I was afraid that he might not remember me.

As I approached the dementia unit, I saw an elderly man with straight white hair starring out a window while eating his lunch. The nurse announced to him that he had a visitor. He looked at me with no expression. Then, the nurse asked him if he recognized me and he said, "she is my daughter." I smiled because his words were sweet music to my ears!

24

*hope*

That day, I matured a little more. I realized that living a full life is all about constant change. However, there are two life seasons that remain the same. We are born to live and we live to die. The paths that we take during our lives are predefined. We make good and bad choices. Our choices will produce an action that can be celebratory or it can cause a negative consequence. My father was born twenty years before me. Although he began his life journey decades before me, I'm certain that he lived a hardy life with little regrets. Our conversation that day was still one directional. However, Joe said that he still loved women and fishing. As he reminisced, his eyes twinkled and his elderly grin actually turned youthful for a moment.

## MAMA

I unapologetically acknowledge that I was raised by a young, single black woman. Our age difference is twenty years. I cannot recall a single day that my mother has not been my supporter. I often thank God because He perfectly created mama for her daughters.

She has a remarkable strength that is outlined with intellect and grace. She has always led by example. As a teenager, I recall her working and attending college so that we could have a well-rounded life. We lacked nothing. During report card time, she was the first to show her grades to her daughters. What an inspiring mother she was and still is today!

Mama was the preferred party host amongst her friends. Therefore, we often had parties or social gatherings at our house. Some were adult dinner parties, while others were teenage parties or a casual elegant tea party. I am certain these activities enhanced my desire to organize social events. To this day, she and I still collaborate and plan events. I'm forever grateful for her encouragement to walk by faith while reaching for the stars.

I've always respected her as my mother and friend. I've been with her on her journey and it has not been an easy walk. However, the challenges she's faced help her to display a mountain of faith with a valley of hope. Today, I salute my mama!

*hope*

# STAIRWAY OF ENCOURAGEMENT

When our children were young adults right out of high school, my husband and I advised them to make their college and career decisions. We encouraged them to select their dreams to follow. We walked them to the stairway and encouraged them to take one step up at a time. We told them that they will encounter obstacles that might hinder them for a moment. When this happens, we encouraged them to self-reflect before moving to the next level. As they complete each step towards the top stair, they need to glance in the direction from which they came. Then, they must acknowledge gratitude for their accomplishment.

# FEED THE HUNGRY PARTY

I celebrated a milestone birthday during the pandemic by having a virtual birthday party with forty guests. I prayed for a successful event! It was not the usual zoom party because there was live entertainment by a Philly R&B Recording Artist and a Brooklyn Deejay.

The party's highlight was a raffle fundraiser to purchase 60 meals at a local food bank. The raffle winner was gracious to pay her gift forward. As a result, we ended up purchasing 1600 meals at the food bank! I share this with you because the initial goal was 60 meals but God blessed us with 1600! Won't He, do it? God's blessings never cease to amaze me!

*hope*

# GRANDMA'S INSPIRATION

I am related to many wise women and am inspired by each of them. One in particular is my maternal grandmother. She had a gentle spirit and had the ability to produce quick, sassy remarks that I define as unique quotes. Whenever she observed me stressed out about something, she quoted scriptures from the bible about how it's easy to worry about tomorrow when we should be focusing on today.

When she was terminally ill, I recall reading scriptures from the bible to her while she laid in her hospital bed. I remember opening the bible to a scripture about how tomorrow will take care of itself. When I read the verse to grandma, she had a calm look on her face. I felt a sense of relief that God chose the perfect moment for me to read the scripture that she had spoken to me so many times.

As I share my thoughts with you, I think about how my grandmother encouraged me to live each day without fear; but with faith. As life would have it, my faith gets tested time after time. There's always drama waiting around the corner. However, prayers have a higher rating than stressful situations and prayers do not have expiration dates.

## FOR THE LOVE OF SIBLINGS

I am blessed to have one sister and three brothers! From a biological perspective, none of us share both parents. My sister and I share the same mother. However, my brothers and I share the same father. As a perfect result, they all share me! As complicated as it may appear, we are siblings! I love them individually and together. This is a perfect example of God's divine plan to create me as their sister. I am grateful that he chose us for each other!

*hope*

# MY INSPIRATIONAL DANCE

As I was recovering from vitamin D deficiency, I developed a desire to do creative dance again. As a teenager, I was in a dance troupe that performed in Fort Lauderdale. So, this new desire to dance was a complete surprise to me.

I've always enjoyed watching praise worship dance performances at church. During a quiet prayer time, I chuckled aloud and said to God, "I am not youthful but I want to dance," and the thought that came to me was a feeling within my soul that I would dance for healing. I understood it to mean that it would be a universal healing. Not just for me but for others.

As a result, I choreographed a dance that I performed at a nursing home for the residents. I told them that I was dancing for healing. The lesson I learned from inspirational dancing is that it does not matter about my age. When I praise worship dance, I'm healing from within. The eyes that see me dance will heal as well.

# PARENTAL GUIDANCE

I have found that it is a full job being a parent. Parenting does not come with one playbook that has to be followed step by step. Parenting is about taking care of your children and providing guidance for them to become productive citizens. There's no perfect way to parent. Every parent will make a mistake in their parenting skills. That's life.

No matter how much a parent strives for perfection, their adult child will make some decisions that will cause consequences. It does not mean that the parent failed at parenting, it means that their adult child took a different path. Every situation will work itself out. One thing I know for sure, you can ask any parent about their adult child and they will give you more information than you need to know. That's because every parent has a story to tell and be heard.

*hope*

# AN AHA MOMENT

I think that it's perfectly fine to describe some of our life experiences to be hilariously funny at times. It can be so funny that you'll need to laugh to the degree that it causes tears to run down your face. Then, you shake your head while grinning from ear to ear. Today, that's me.

I'm thinking about the times that I made a complete fool out of myself by trying to cheer someone up. It was a great feeling to not have to think about how ridiculous we might look to others. At this moment, I feel grateful to reflect on laughter because it's good, free therapy for the soul.

## BECOMING MIMI

What an amazing moment to witness the birth of your grandchild! That's the day that my daughter gained the title of mom. As I watched her give birth, I found myself in awe of becoming a Mimi. There I was assuming the role of a wiser generation to the one I was just leaving. At that moment, my life changed forever.

*hope*

# WEDDING DANCES

I recall two dance partners in my life to help me celebrate major milestones. The first dancer was my father when I was a bride. Back then, the father and daughter did not choreograph a special dance for the reception. We danced a perfect father and daughter dance! Since we lived states apart, we did not see each other often. In fact, my wedding reception is the only time I remember dancing with my father in a lifetime.

Decades later, I found myself dancing with my son at his wedding reception. Although dances are now a choreographed entertainment for some receptions, the slow ballad that we selected was the perfect song that did not require a rehearsal. That was a defining moment for me to recognize my son as a newly married man. I was proud of the person he had become.

In both situations, practicing did not guarantee perfection. We danced our special dance with confidence and style. We accomplished a priceless bond that only a parent and child can enjoy while all eyes are on them. While they were two different milestones in my life, the outcome was the same. I am grateful for those two memorable dances that are engraved in my soul.

# HOUSE FOR SALE

Whatever life throws your way, you need to intercept the negative thoughts with hope and faith. I remember when we listed our starter home on the real estate market. We had approximately fifty families look at our house. I remember thinking that something must be wrong with the house or the price wasn't right.

One day, our realtor informed us that we received a "sight unseen" purchase offer. The family was relocating and needed to purchase a house right away. The doubt that we previously had was erased with a blessing. It was God's plan for us to be patient and wait for the perfect family that he'd selected to buy our house. The family did not counter-offer the purchase price. To this day, we acknowledge this as a blessing from God.

*hope*

# UNCONDITIONAL LOVE

Every family's relationship is different. I'm blessed to have a family with unconditional love. We all are imperfect people that love and respect each other for better or worse. What you see is what you get and what you get is genuine love from one generation to the other. There's a lot of encouraging conversations when we get together. I'm describing all my family members.

I must say that God gifted me with the perfect family for me to marry into. They embraced me immediately when my future husband took me to meet them. I almost felt like I was a long-lost relative when I first walked into their home. That welcoming feeling has lasted a lifetime.

The calendar years come and go. In order for families to remain healthy, we must continue the family gatherings as well as periodically check the well-being of family members. I think it is good to know family history so that each generation has knowledge of our hope and resilience. It's also essential for us to know our family health history as well. When you combine the history of knowledge with unconditional love, you've got a strong family foundation.

# THE QUEEN

I decided to try out the pageantry competitions when I was in my early twenties. I remember the disappointment I felt when I lost the Miss Black Gainesville Pageant. I'd prepared in every way. I had worked out so that my swimsuit would fit amazing. I completed mock interview questions and worked tirelessly on the talent competition that was a poem written by a friend.

The poem was about a young lady's grief when her mother passed away. It was an emotional poem that I'd perfected and could shed tears within 20 seconds. I had not planned to have any props except for carrying a dozen of roses. However, at the last minute, I changed the props for the talent scene so that it would appear more realistic. I was able to get a local funeral home to donate flower stands and a casket as props.

The auditorium was full to capacity. I was confident that my performance would award me as a first or second place winner. But fate would have it differently. Sometimes it does not pay to second guess yourself by changing something that you'd perfected for several months. As a perfectionist, I strived to make it better when it was already a very good presentation that did not need additional props to get the message across. It just needed talent and I'd recited poems all my life, so I knew how to perform.

I knew it was a mistake when no one in the audience applauded the performance. It was quite apparent that the prop did not settle well with the audience. In addition, I was later told that one of the judges had recently experienced a loss and it affected the votes for my talent competition. That was one of the most humiliating moments in my life. Although my family and friends were supportive, I was extremely embarrassed at the outcome of that experience on stage. For someone that's a perfectionist, this was a devastating experience for me.

*hope*

A year later, I was hesitant to compete in the Miss Black Fort Lauderdale Pageant. However, I decided to approach it with a different mindset. I needed to overcome whatever constraints I had developed after losing the Gainesville Pageant. I was determined to display poise while having fun. The swimsuit competition was fair, we all wore the same type of bathing suit. The mock interview questions were easy because I'd been in a previous pageant before. The talent skit that I selected was one that required very little props. I just needed to work on my delivery to the audience.

When the stage lights turned on, I was in the zone. I was confident and happy on the stage. The outcome was unexpected; I won two titles that night (Miss Black Fort Lauderdale / Miss Black Broward County). I clearly did not expect to win. I participated to win back the confidence I'd lost at the Miss Black Gainesville Pageant. It can take a painful loss to humble us. That night, I developed a renewed sense of confidence while having fun.

## THE PROPOSAL

It was a hot summer night drive on Fort Lauderdale Beach as we passed by the bars that were in full capacity with patrons enjoying the happy hour time. We decided to park the car to listen to the waves serenading a natural symphony of music to our ears. I had an inkling feeling that he was going to proposed to me. We'd discussed marriage a few times in the past.

As we listened and watch the tides roll back and forth, he showed me the most beautiful ring and asked me to be his wife. I'm glad that we were sitting in the car because I probably would have dropped the ring in the sand when I said yes. That summer night on the beach was the perfect setting for him to propose to me, his soulmate and best friend. We've been inseparable ever since.

*hope*

# THE SERENADE

We attended a music festival that was headlined with one of our favorite song artists. Our eyes immediately lit up when he began to sing our favorite song! We grabbed each other and walked into the main aisle. We danced while he sang that song. We didn't care that there were thousands of people in our proximity. As the performer sang each verse, we sang with him and held each other. As we were serenaded, it felt like we were the only ones there.

*"Select your path and keep right on walking."* Michelle R. Palmer

41

# EPILOGUE

* ★ *

The purpose of completing this book is because I'm entering a different phase of my life. I thank God for my health and the relationships I have had with many of you for a lifetime! To my new supporters, thank you for allowing me to share my walk by faith with you.

Everyone has a story to tell. For me, I wanted to share it with you because I believe this will motivate others to follow their dreams. I've desired to publish a book my entire life but always let circumstances get in the way. Guess what? This time, I didn't allow self-doubt to get in the way.

I had a vision to listen to my inner self and write down whatever came to my mind. I believe that everyone has good, bad, beautiful and ugly experiences during their journey. I'm no different than the next person. However, my story is now published.

I hope that you enjoyed the reading and I look forward to sharing more of my journey with you. I've developed a writer's craving like there is no tomorrow. But we know that with God's will, each tomorrow will become a today!

*"I yearn to write a passage that will peel back layers of emotion to show my inner self and motivate others to follow their dreams."*

Michelle R. Palmer

*hope*

Photo Courtesy of L.Yvonne Reid Garvin

43

Photo Courtesy of L.Yvonne Reid Garvin

*hope*

Photo Courtesy of Dr. DiAnna Montfort

Photo Courtesy of Dr. DiAnna Montfort

Photo Courtesy of Dr. DiAnna Montfort

hope

# ABOUT THE AUTHOR

★ ✯ ★

Michelle R. Palmer, affectionately known as Micki, is an upcoming writer that shares inspirational essays in this classic book. A native Floridian, Michelle talks from the heart with an inspiring quality. An avid beach lover, it's no surprise that she writes in her journal while sitting under her beach umbrella.

Michelle married her college sweetheart and they have two adult children. She's a grandmother that enjoys going to live concerts, sporting events and loves organizing special events. She also enjoys bargain hunting while conducting retail therapy. Her favorite colors are royal purple and teal.

Michelle achieved her undergraduate degrees from the University of Florida and graduate degree from the University of Phoenix. She has worked in telecom, health care and power energy industries in the areas of project management, technical writing and IT purchasing/procurement. Michelle is a member of Zeta Phi Beta Sorority Incorporated, where she has held leadership roles at the local and state levels.

This book is to be embraced and cherished by looking into the soul of a survivor with an enriched faith. Her descriptions of humbleness, hope and endurance gracefully glide through the path of where she's been with a determination of better tomorrow.

She hopes that a reader is encouraged to not give up on faith but to embrace the challenges with resilience. Michelle Palmer's latest work offers sincerity on every page.

**Website:** mickimichellethewriter.com

# BOOK SYNOPSIS

— ★ ★ ★ —

The author describes how we often worry about the things that will eventually work themselves out. People can get caught up on worrying about the tomorrows when they really need to focus on the todays. The author candidly shares her journey of finding hope, joy and faith as it relates to self-esteem, relationships, health and overcoming losses.

This book is to be embraced and cherished by looking into the soul of a survivor with an enriched faith. The author plants descriptions of humbleness, hope and endurance while she gracefully glides through the path of where she's been with a determination of a better tomorrow. The author writes to encourage readers to not give up on faith, but to embrace the challenges with resilience.

*hope*

Made in the USA
Columbia, SC
30 October 2021